THE NIGHTFIELDS

Also by Joanna Klink

EXCERPTS FROM A SECRET PROPHECY

RAPTUS

CIRCADIAN

THEY ARE SLEEPING

THE NIGHTFIELDS

Joanna Klink

PENGUIN POETS

PENGUIN BOOKS

An imprint of Penguin Random House LLC
penguinrandomhouse.com

LIBRARY OF CONGRESS CATALOGING-IN-PUBLICATION DATA
Names: Klink, Joanna, 1969– author.
Title: The nightfields / Joanna Klink.
Description: [New York] : Penguin Books, [2020] | Series: Penguin poets |
Identifiers: LCCN 2019054193 (print) | LCCN 2019054194 (ebook) |
ISBN 9780143135395 (paperback) | ISBN 9780525507062 (ebook)
Subjects: LCSH: Loss (Psychology)—Poetry | LCGFT: Poetry.
Classification: LCC PS3561.L5 N54 2020 (print) | LCC PS3561.L5 (ebook) |
DDC 811/.54—dc23
LC record available at https://lccn.loc.gov/2019054193
LC ebook record available at https://lccn.loc.gov/2019054194

Set in ITC Galliard Std

for my father, William Hermann Klink

ACKNOWLEDGMENTS

Some of these poems have appeared under different titles, in other forms.

And sometimes sky, Hammered copper, In the ease of winds and sun are reprinted from THE ELOQUENT POEM, edited by Elise Paschen (Persea Books, 2019).

Lines from *The Infinities* are included in Saul Melman's "Untitled" (Paint, linen, cotton, and abaca), 2019.

A PUBLIC SPACE   *The Infinities*

ACADEMY OF AMERICAN POETS   *On Falling (Blue Spruce), New Year*

THE ADROIT JOURNAL   *Evenings and Days, Statue from Antiquity*

BENNINGTON REVIEW   *Portrait in Summer*

BOSTON REVIEW   *On Surmising*

BOULEVARD   *Crossland, The Dusks, On Kingdoms, On Standing Still*

THE COMMON   *What have you, in such indignation, become, The birds have disappeared into trees, If you have grieved you have loved, But you are unscathed*

CRAZYHORSE   *A Friendship, On Mercy*

HARVARD REVIEW   *What if this darkness, We were born, Dark summer grass, Long days*

KENYON REVIEW   *Almanac, The Devotions, Millennia. Dry winds, Who are we, on the ground, Centuries, signal flares, Dark blue, Ankerite glints in the ground, Black sky soaked with ghost-violet, Time of wind, time of dust, time of sky*

NEW ENGLAND REVIEW   *We were weightless, Against the white walls, There is no almanac, Desert heat rippling the dusk, Power lines shine from the rain, Underground fountains and grottos, It is easy, It is late*

NEW REPUBLIC   *They were never yours*

PARIS REVIEW   *Cancer (Prayer for my father)*, *And what did you see*, *Dusk,
electrical veil, Quiet, liquid pearl*

POETRY FOUNDATION   *Elegy*

TIN HOUSE   *On Diminishment, On Abiding*

Grateful acknowledgment to the University of Montana, Williams College,
Civitella Ranieri, the Bogliasco Foundation, the MacDowell Colony, Yaddo,
the American Academy in Rome Visiting Artists and Scholars Program, the
Trust of Amy Lowell, and the John Simon Guggenheim Memorial Foundation.

My deepest thanks to Paul Slovak, and to these exceptional readers: Michele
Glazer, John D'Agata, Patrick Hutchins, David Greenberg, Mark Guziel,
Matthew Kreider, and David Baker.

Abiding love to Saul Melman, Emily Hughes, Julie Rae O'Connor, Andy Laue,
Honor Moore, Mary Szybist, Anna Maria Hong, Mira Tanna, Cammy
Brothers, Michelle Berenfeld, David Deschamps, Bennett Singer, Dana
Prescott, Irma Boom, Deb Busch, Steve Klink, Mia Žnidarič, and to my
mother, Judith Klink.

CONTENTS

There is no masterwork
I walked for an hour
And if it is true
Only for this

What if this darkness
And what did you see
We were born
Dark summer grass
What have you, in such indignation, become
The birds have disappeared into trees
But you are unscathed
We were weightless
Quiet, liquid pearl
And sometimes sky
Desert heat rippling the dusk
There is no almanac
We seek the dark
Dusk, electrical veil
Against the white walls
They were never yours
Long days
If you have grieved you have loved
Power lines shine from the rain
Millenia. Dry winds
Who are we, on the ground
Centuries, signal flares
Underground fountains and grottos
Dark blue
It is easy
Hammered copper
Ankerite glints in the ground
It is late
In the ease of winds and sun
Black sky soaked with ghost-violet
Time of wind, time of dust, time of sky

When I go toward you
it is with my whole life.

Rainer Maria Rilke, *The Book of Hours*

THE NIGHTFIELDS

THE INFINITIES

I don't know when it began,
the will to sort moment
from moment, to hold
on by saying I can't
care about the red maple
stripped of color, I choose
the rain disappearing
at my feet. I choose
this friend to love, the deep
blacks of summer. Abandon
the rest. I am unable to
picture anything so whole
it doesn't crush what's
missing. Is it my body across
many seasons turning
already a little to bone,
or the slow stars precisely
set in depths so vast
the sky is just a dome
within falling domes.
How is the snowfield
scattered with dry leaves already
a pavilion of twilight. And my arms
just a motion in the great
soundlessness of sky.

I have traded childhood
exuberance for fragile
acts. I will slip into
corner tables just to watch
people speak. I love the way
they lean into each other
or stretch back with the bluespun
languor of an evening, lights
strung up on the wood
ceiling to mimic the lift of
stars. There are no
empty hopes. But knowing
what to hope for is steady
work. What was ever
so important to you you left
your daily life to heed it?
I don't even know what
breathes in the dark hills
outside this town. Some
mornings the roads almost
float, the weeds in the fields
wiry fistfuls of sun. What
were you looking out for?
What did you dismiss
along the way.

Because we live we are granted
names, streams, shocks of
heat, murmuring summers.
All the days you have
ever breathed are swallows
shooting between trees.
When the wind pushes
branches in and out of
shade it is an opening,
as every small gesture
toward another person is
incomprehensibly alive.
Will you be part of the
stoneless passage? When life
starts to take things away
will you grow very still
beneath the larch
or feel the slow flight of birds
across your body.
The bright key of morning.
The bay fanned with foam.

ON FALLING (BLUE SPRUCE)

Dusk fell every night. Things
fall. Why should I
have been surprised.

Before it was possible
to imagine my life
without it, the winds

arrived, shattering air
and pulling the tree
so far back its roots,

ninety years, ripped
and sprung. I think
as it fell it became

unknowable. Every day
of my life now I cannot
understand. The force

of dual winds lifting
ninety years of stillness
as if it were nothing,

as if it hadn't held every
crow and fog, emptying
night from its branches.

The needles fell. The pinecones
dropped every hour
on my porch, a constant

irritation. It is enough
that we crave objects,
that we are always

looking for a way
out of pain. What is beyond
task and future sits right

before us, endlessly
worthy. I have planted
a linden, with its delicate

clean angles, on a plot
one tenth the size. Some change
is too great.

Somewhere there is a field,
white and quiet, where a tree
like this one stands,

made entirely of
hovering. Nothing will
hold me up like that again.

ON KINGDOMS

Who is ever at home in oneself.
Land without mercy. Interstates
set flickering by night. When I speak to you
I can feel a storm falling blackly to the roads,
the pelting rains the instant they
hit. Devotion is full of arrows.
Most weeks I am no more than the color of the walls
in the room where we sit, or I am blind to clocks,
restless, off-guard, accomplice to the weathers
that burn and flee, foamless, across a sky
that was my past, that is
what I was. I am always too close.
I am not sure I will ever be
wholly alive. Still—we are faithful.
Small birds hook their flights into the fog.
The heat crosses in shoals over these roads
and this evening the cottonwoods may sway
with that slow darkgold wind
beyond all urgency. I am listening to you.

ON DIMINISHMENT

The hours I wake
into are not empty
but the sounds

have grown smaller.
Vertical drop of a
spider thread,

its slow glass
passage. A breath
beneath rooms full of paper.

I am, since you
turned away from me,
the most delicate

book. And I think:
I made myself kind.
I put things down for you.

I wish it had been
quiet enough
then to say: I am sorry.

We are sorry.
We take all our love back.

*

And here, in the month
of my birth, light

crosses the walls
for hours until dark blue
summer dusk

surrounds me. Each day
I return unnoticed to my home.

But at night I hear the cool
roads across town,

see rain on the hands
of a child who lingered a while
in the yard.

Somewhere insects
are brushing the lamps and stars

have slipped in their dome
over us—their positions
fixed, intact, and perfect.

*

It is hard to shape
oneself to oneself.

Who are you?
What is here?

Kites above a muddy field,
your body windless
as it watches.

If too much has
happened to you,
whom do you tell?

It is costly
to love without
giving over to love.

It is costly
to look too much
after yourself.

*

I was no more than
bones, cloud—I was only

rain floating. Some days
more stone than road.

Some days the high white
flash of a fountain.

I was only a country,
a body folding nightly

into its tides. I could not
expect anything.

I was wood
without knowing.

*

It is possible to love
without purpose.

It is possible to walk
far into another
and find only

yourself. If there is a right
action of the throat,

it is to say: I tried,
I stayed a long time there.

You can let the whole
of those years go un-
answered. The stairwell,

the porch swing, the reading
chair where I'd greet you,

looking away, as if my
arriving and leaving

were never really
part of the pleasure.

The most fragile thought
can live inside you for months,
and you carry on

as if it weren't real.
You can speed up so fast

you can't even hear
the ruin in the bell,

the slip of pain inside
trust, the ownerless
nothingness you have now

come to share with
someone you
once found so good.

GIVENS

We were given a book, and the book stripped
the world down to dirt and to rain, captivity,
color. The sky must have followed us
into the grove where we sat and felt happy
that the grasses were empty, the olive trees empty.
We were given some salt, a warehouse, a river,
and when we rose the birds stayed
with us all night. If you were given a burden,
if you were given a rock, an omen, would you know
it too could go missing, it too could be broken.
If you knew just what you were given, would the ache
break out of it. Would it help you. Would you open.

You were given a book and inside the book
was a road leading to orchards and snow,
tiny dustings of sun. You must have
followed the flashlights and felt you'd been offered
proof, or else hope, which itself is not simple.
There are great bays in the thoughts of old men,
there are winds that break leaves into cool wheels of shade.
You were given a latchkey, an x-ray, you were given
the means to fly and the means not to crawl.
Why would you even listen for trains or pay attention
to branches. Why would you root into yourself
when the rain could, any moment, coax light into color.

I was given a book. I was given two bells
to make a pact with the air. I was given
the smell of new rain, a small stack of paper,
some gold leaf and glue. If you were given some yarn,
some wire, if you were given a whole night of snow,
would you even know how to hold it.
Go easy on that old red oak. Go easy
on the man at the corner who just asked for money,
he is probably hungry, and what would he do
if he were given a boat, a breeze, and what would he
usher into himself if he thought life would help him.

ALMANAC

Better to be awake at night in sympathy with clocks
than to wander vaguely
    through days.
Better to feel a hush in the yard.
To cultivate a faith in strangers,
in air and evening, in spots of sun
    rising up the high oaks.
They are the harbor lights returned to you,
    the people you loved returned to you,
    the long sleep of pilgrims.
If you are deprived of hope
to still sometimes feel its power.
And the tides at night rippling back from
    cold sand—to sense them
even if you have never seen them.
We are fine rain and shining streets.
We throw away things of great value and feel confused.
Seize upon the smallest arguments and call them huge.
(Some days I am small beyond measure.
Some days I am the fence the field the trees.)

———————————————————

Were they important to you, the calm eyes of the cattle,
the statues and their motionless
    hearts. The parks residing
deep in you. Was the wind turning white
important to you, the scarves in their sweeps
    around floating throats, dozing
    restaurants at noon. A clatter of dishes,
foggy sheets in the eyes of commuters,
the airplanes gliding down through white dusk.
The ground doves in their murmuring feathers.

The cements of abandoned lots.
Church bells are moving across old hills
and if you don't believe in churches
you could believe in their awe, in the unrecognizable
agates in their cemetery
    plots. What will you admit
    into your life? Will that station be
held by you—to be alive as you're living.

No more stalemates of feeling.
No more bitterness from the throats
of those lucky enough to live
    where it is still possible to hear sounds
not shaped by cars.
(And if I have been scarred, it is because I gave up
those woods and the long
nightfall of color.)
Better to let the snows press
down against land.
Better to discourage the future by making no plans.
    No plans!—better to
backtrack and distrust than to prize.
Prize your day these hours won't happen again.
Prize the person who touches you in the simplest way
    against all disappointment.
Better to collapse into what you love
than to ask for so little. Do not make progress,
    do not be courteous. From here
you can begin your day again, more grateful than
thankless. Unprepared as we are
for what's
    coming. Unprepared as we are to lose
anything. As I was to lose you.

The wind this evening
      whistles into the nightweeds

November drops the changes
      upon us
The short days overcome us
A darkness laced between houses
      We become skeletal
      We reach for whatever
      feels like light

And how could you ever
get what you want
when you would need to believe in
      something other than
the past—friends, mornings, walks,
      the spindling branchwork
      of cold trees—

But this was daylight
This was *hope*
      We had *begun again*

The hours of more than three years
captive to a plot that still
      makes no sense
as the sky sheeted white
      as if burning or lucent
above a street now impassable
and a regret so profound I cannot
      speak it—the way we say
      This my only life

Or the way we will not forget
what has happened to us.

EVENINGS AND DAYS

Having woken many days I still
can't account for
myself, at night on the floor
with books spread
around me, spines black
below the lamps. I read
about the houses of the rich
and the poor, a woman thinking,
a woman combing her hair, the great
pain that would come to a young
man. You can hold
an umbrella above your head
and look out at deep
calm, rain drumming to
nothing. Walking through
traffic the steady roughness of
engines, and in dusk or late
evening the grasses seem
darker than trees. If you stare
at something for a long
time you may come to
trust it. That thin
shadow of wire fence through
dense heat was your life.
And even so you stepped past it.

There were evenings when the iced
air softened our throats, days
when there was such
light on the snow you could barely
see it. There are always
moments when no one
speaks. In summer my friends
lead their kids across cement saying
Look. An airplane floats past, a bike
netted with baskets. Their children,
always moving, understand
the absence of wind. I admire
how they rush into space,
use their arms to make the kiosk
grand. At the park my friend's daughter
a shining bead on the field
as she kicks the ball, abacus of
laughter. We hardly know
who we are but we go on
living. A man I loved has let his
heart go slack. A city I loved
is a stack of properties.
There is always the deep
need of something gone.

Of course there were days of
extraordinary clearness, the sun
casting beams through wires of
rain, and you caught
the tired eye-muscles
of the clerk but because it was
late did not bother to say a brief
word. I am awake
but unable to recognize
the route, though I feel a slight
rise in the earth in the public
park and dearly love the benches
that hold the old men.
When I was young I wanted
the giddy pain that came with
love but now would give
anything for understanding,
one person sensing
the other, and joy
that rushes in for no reason.
When the morning is quiet
I can hear someone trimming
those trees, a young girl smokes
as she waits for the bus.
Somewhere in myself she is
completely at ease. Clouds
seem to be rising from the west,
the end of who we are comes
towards us—strange new
machines and ruined lands—
and though the people I saw shared
some of my fears we never
spoke. I was more
diminished than I knew. What
is it that brings me to you.

ON STANDING STILL

In the afterdusk
I waited by the street,
for a few minutes free of

       engines. Gold light
       from the awnings
       came on. The color

seemed, like the sound,
to be an ancient order
thrown over

       the blankness of
       standing. I stood.
       I waited.

And soon mistakes swept
through me, friends
I had abandoned,

       each failure to return.
       There is a way to live

not racked by guesswork—
simply to pivot

       and claim one direction,
       to make your path
       felt. If you hold

completely still, the clock-
gears are tipping in near-
silence, the darkness

rolling out across
the freeways. All the flowing
lights without warmth.

*

If I wait by the white
piano keys, I can hear
my brother playing,

the scattered bits of
darkness assemble into
morning notes. Hold

fast—the upsweep of his
hands is an ease of
chords and luck to

remember. I am here now,
by these salvaged doors.

I claim a view of the yard
without speed, one that
stays for hours

with the flares of sun
between high oaks.
If I am signaling,

it is to the crow-swept
ground, the chance to
break with a habit of

days. Belonging
nowhere yet at this
late hour of life,

I hold an account
so quiet the room's
inlit softness spins

     around me. But if I
     jolt into place, it will
     be by the grace of

some other order,
the one that brings
sudden winds—

     and ice, and sunlight,
     and gold leaf.

        *

A mountain darkness,
the swinging lights
of a town I only know

     I have to leave.
     I am without goals or
     plans. In the morning

I latch my hands
to a new trust: steady

     myself by the door,
     reach for the roof

of my car. Against
the backdrop of earth

       I only know life is
       brisk—will take away
       what one loves most.

How else would we
learn but by force.

       When we drove the
       backroads and the fields

flashed between trees,
what was shown to us

       was that the land
       would not last,

and our bodies with it—
bearers of names,
headstrong, fighting

       defeat as we half-
       close our eyes into
       the breeze of a

moving car, the dry
autumn air that carries
hours of sunlight

       in it, whole slow
       afternoons, and orchards.

THE NETS

Who is that   in the old photo
Jeans and ripped cardigan   hair pulled

loosely back   Who is that beside you
Someone who mattered   in a night

swaying with lights   What happened
to the long hours in which you lived

Slow blue dawns   patterns of
rain   What wrestled through you

Furious choices   black tunnels of thought
What gathered   inside the evening's

sheer winds   Perhaps a few clouds
the bird's smokedark trill

What were you   unable to say
Burdens of others   the disfigurement

within disease   how it feels to lose
conviction   Where are your devotions

Still arriving   the spring-action inside
ships needles fountains

What were you not   able to find
Simplicity   or enough patience

enough hours   What leapt up
when you looked   The directness of his

eyes   their bright brown core light
What did your throat do

What did your hands   What was
durable corruptible   What closed

the distance between forms
Whom did you touch   kinetic

When did life   seem to run out
Did you understand   the enormity

of the change inside that   bleaching heat
When were you blinded   by a sense of

endurance   What quiet fell
into the long roads   What was love

Everything we could not keep
What was hate   Deadness and havoc

inside the capacity to act   What is tenderness
The soft names for air   What did you crave

Woodsmoke against the screen-door
his collarbone or bending spine

What was in you   Meshes of silver
What was in us   Time on earth

CROSSLAND

I crossed the streets at five,
past the park, the wind knocking at swings.
Or I was unable to pass by—
children at the slides, a few dogs flying at sticks,
the murmur of a peace that is
constant in this world and impossible to keep.

I go on trying. I could call out or not.
I could try to stop their suffering
across those months or I could not.
It kept on without me—
I made no mark, I saw no gate,
there were no clues no games no breeze.
I tried to drive into my skull some right
reprieve, and when I could not,
held on to sleep, I winced
and turned away, I let my heart
thin as it opened out, I went again
and again into the moods of late afternoons,
I walked through a recurrence of equal dusks,
admitting no other presence except for them
who were gone, my friends, I hoped
every hope for them and there was nothing
for that hope to catch on, I wondered
if there might, some hour, appear an element
to shelter and bring far into winter
such path-lights that do not tell you where to go
but nevertheless, against the blue night, burn.
I asked not how long but who am I
that walks in this direction. What then is mine.
These sore lungs, my bones
drifting out across the pavement
as if it could be made right by time

and voyaging, and the sky offer some sign
beyond its cloud-swept
motion—a pardon.

Please. Give us birds.
A light unto a world. An undistorted,
ancient ornament—some swift way
out of the earth.
Where the stones are laid.
Where we are laid.

THE DUSKS

As one thing is entrance unto another
the dark moon becomes new.
A sense of wind between trees,
a dense lace of frost holding the grass
back. If there are stars, they are lashed to clouds
that pass as slowly as thoughts above the pines,
    the highway, the shattered
hillsides. Dusk spread hours ago
as the air thinned, froze, as the invisible moon
    rose. Moon of battered moths.
Moon of chance bravery.
Moon of the hoped-for hollowed-out throat.

*

For a long time I have loved them,
    their wages and ravages.
The dusks are tides unto evening.
They are blue snows to bristle and hard ground.
Winter-born even in the beaded summer minutes,
bafflements unto outline, shapeless weights
pushing the canyons into their original
    depths. For a long time by myself,
as they lit with quiet the thick frost-
fields. In preparation of moons, in preparation of lanterns.
For a long time I kept their particular rivers close,
drawing into myself at the blurring hour,
the hour of wide blue drift.
And night eventually brings stillness,
which means tomorrow there is a chance
I might find myself

less alone, or at least
more equal to the stiff branches of the maple,
    this dog loping past me.
More equal to the useless stars
above the meadow in darkness.
Wind of boats.
Wind of each black dawn.

As one thing is entrance unto another
the birch tree is a pleat, a curtain, a crop—
a cloud of thunder unwinding in dark silver,
leaving behind the day-ordered world, declaring
    This region you live in is more than yours
    More than what you have lost in your lifetime.
    More than you could ever hope to gain.

                        *

For a long time by myself, sleeping
and rising and falling into bed again, every hoped-for
chance encounter a dim reminder of my own
    compasslessness. Asleep
in the blue of ardor,
asleep in greed.
What will I gain.
What can the world do for me.

A feeling is a grave into which you sink,
forgetting it was ever a grave, forgetting even your own
    ill-equipped unhappiness.
And how could you be brought back
to the slow-flowing change—
and how could you ever
unfold again? On the earth

into which you were set
   without understanding.
Alongside the farmlands reverting to marsh.
Alongside the birds. Who cannot travel
further north or higher up.

THE DEVOTIONS

Have you been there all along,
the softness of shadow in taverns,
the barely-moving air around
century-old trees. I had never
needed to look.
Now even a bird
struggling to stay in flight
is neither weight nor
pain. When I move toward you
it is with everything I have lived,
emptied out. Like the deer,
whose bodies thread at evening
into the deepening grass.

Only for this do you
return to us, our calls of hunger,
our driving need.
Voices from the radio
all day in warning. At night
the low whir of snowplows
blowing open the path.
It is so easy to lose one's direction,
to spread a confusion that began
only in oneself. Outside
the snow seems
indistinguishable from wind.
Without so much as moving
I touched the window.
What I could not know
came to me.

CANCER (PRAYER FOR MY FATHER)

Far into fever, attached by cords
to the clicking machines, he sleeps
in a bed in a room not his own.
People enter and pass like ghost-blown
fogs. He is a slow walk
with limbs that recently gave way.
He is part of the blue snowfall.
He is very small, sitting on a curb
with skinny legs next to an elegant
aunt. He is not yet born.
He travels to meet the relatives
in Maulbronn and feels the lifting darkness
sunk in his chair at night, thinking.
He is intensely wrong, obstinate and generous,
the one who never seems to grieve,
sweaters and wine and violas locked in
air. You say: he too cannot be found again,
he too asks only for more aliveness
and time. The room is like every room
in that house, sterile and never silent,
but sometimes birds drop into the air
above his sleep and coast for hours
on loose currents. There is no fire
but weathered blood and skin, a threaded
endurance, the peace
of placing your body in the hands
of those who might know,
the voices saying Have you eaten,
What could you have done.
The frost in your eyes is melting or stays
stitched. The fragile instruments of bodies
step into the room and out, the machine
counts two three four, and part of who you are

travels into the glass hallways that are filling
with warm light. He walks
only for so long. He approaches each sorrow
and lets it fall. He is unaccountably at ease
for just a single instant, he is
not an important name, he is the crucial man
inside the waning fever, the one who taught you
to care, he follows the deep tasks
even as he surrenders, one by one, his body's
dignities. He is the concert of bright strings,
the sudden gentleness of moss,
the tyrant opinion, a confusion of medications.
His mind is a room casting infinite love
from four walls. My beautiful father,
you carried me out into the day of my life
and let me stand on earth with affection
and force. Why should we fear our disappearance.

ON ABIDING

I never wanted
to be awash in

agreement, I never
wanted to argue or

agonize, only to listen
for the rain blown

against glass, sense
who you are

when you are alone but
with me. Present,

the way a birch
late at night
is present to wind.

*

Only I wanted you
next to me
in a sleeping

curve of heat. It seemed
I was always
misplacing you.

But I loved every
part, eyelashes

and limbs, the way you
leapt into the day.

To want a simple life
might mean
to have given up

on expectation.
It could mean

that faith is easily
crushed, that something

as easy as crossing
the street at dusk

is suddenly too physical,
too narrow, too
empty, too hard,

too rich, too small,
too soon.

                      *

If I could see
through the rains,
the liquid trees,

quarrel only for a
moment, never be
rushed. Stop

completely at the river's
lightflutter and wait
until it passes

and feel that quiet
which is the sound

of hawk and
cloud—to make
good of what you have,

to feel the air press
around you and not regret
the loss of you—

the windows of the
night-trains filling with
metal dusk—snow

turning back to rain,
the underside

of everything you have ever
cared for, unsparing

days and nights,
the plain evening,

the uncertainty, the hard work,
the courageous happiness,

the suffering, to see it, to stay
alive, to hope, to hope

for more, to act,
to crave, to reach for,
to let ourselves be

graced, to leave behind
made things, luminous things,
cool trails of fire,

to tap and then step back,
falling silent, to risk an
opening, to find time

to be nowhere and lost
and to love. If we
can. If we do.

. . . . .

NEW YEAR

We woke to the darkness before our eyes,
unable to take the measure of the loss.
Who are they. What are we. What have we
    abandoned to arrive with such violence at this hour.
In answer we drew back, covered our ears
with our hands to the heedless victory, or vowed,
    as I did, into the changed air, never to consent.
But it was already too late, too late for the unfarmed fields,
the men by the station, the park swings, the parking lots,
    the ground water, the doves—too late for dusk
falling in summer, chains of glass lakes
    mingled into dawn, the color of corals, the neighbors,
the first drizzle on an empty street, cafeterias and stockyards,
young men asking twice a day for
    work. Too late for hope. Too far along
to meet a country, a people, its annihilating need.

Because the year is new and the great change
already underway, we concede a thousandfold
    and feel, harder than the land itself,
a complicity for everything we did not see
or comprehend: cynicism borne of raw despair,
long-cultivated hatreds, the promises of leaders
traveling like cool silence through the dark.
My life is here, in this small room, and like you
    I am waiting to know—but there is no time
to wait for what has happened.
What does the future ask of me,
those who won't have enough to eat by evening,
those whose disease will now take hold—
    and the decades that carry past me once I've died,

generations of children, the suffering that is never solved,
the heat over the earth, its marshes,
    its crowded towers, its unbreathable night air.
I would open my hand from the wrist,
step outside, not lose nerve.
Here is the day, still to be lived.
We do not fully know what we do.
But the trains depart the stations, traffic lurches
    and stalls, a highway crew has paused.
Desert sun softens the first color of the rock.
Who governs now governs by grievance and old scores,
    but we compass our worth,
prepare to do the work not our own,
and feel, past the scorn in his eyes, the burden
in the torso of a stranger, draw close to the sick,
    the weak, the women without jobs, the twelve-year-old
facing spite half-tangled into sleep, the panic
tightening inside everyone who has been told to go,
I will help you although I do not know you,
and strive not to look away, be unwilling to profit,
    an ache inside that endless effort,
a slowed-down summons not from those
whose rage is lit by greed—we *do not consent*—
but the ones who wake without prospect,
those who don't speak, cannot recover,
    like the old woman at the counter, the helpless father
who, like you, gets no more than his one life.

NIGHT SKY

What if this darkness is no mirror, no scar. The sound
of night only copper greening. There you are. Above you,
the stars thicken—marshless, measureless. Dry winds
with no source. No lamps deepen the rooms, and to enter
is to flicker against the burnt lunar plane. What if your eyes
are only ghost forests through which veins of blood
stream—what if what you want has only ever been
night, thirst, power lines and red clay, the moving of tunnels
inside your body. Watchman of the hour, you have
become the hour. Everything you hoped was already above you.

And what did you see, sequoia-quiet, looking out at black
night. No islands, no kings or corridors of fury.
But the districts where we were born, a few icy stars,
the moon's beaming chalk thirst. Above the Painted Desert,
the air rustles at your wrists, pulls away from the long
industry on land, up into those far lights. A vast ordinance,
unspoken, with no need to be spoken. Those who
did not have to die. Yourself, and all you loved.

We were born into deathbed photos and charred trees.
Swallows, barns, coats-of-arms. And cannot say
why we were put here, cannot say what we should do.
The oceans of the earth emollient gold, rising powers
flung back into ravenous depths. The deserts blackrubied
nightsands. And still we hoard and lay blame,
we take what we need. Races murder races for land
without mercy and dawn is never withheld. There is a heat
born in you that outlasts you, there are burning circuits of
stars. Where is your life? After all, we have seen the riches.
We have known of each other at every hour.

Dark summer grass. Lightning bugs in their slow
flashing. The night above you was more in you
than your breath, the stars always shifting in your chest.
How many days rippled through you until they were
years, they were suddenly a life—shadows of roses
or shadows of buildings, months of sickness, lost keys.
A neighbor you didn't greet. We are coming and going,
nightstreets and dawnstreets, the blurred mineral ground
we walk on. Just before death, no one speaks with hatred.
Above you, the nightclouds race and then slow,
a beetle burrows into work. Your arms are the quiet
inside trust. Your hands as fragile as snow.

What have you, in such indignation, become. Dusty—
a vaulted interior echoing with air, envy, blood.
Vanity's steady hum. Each wrong done to you
a gate that opens forever into storm. Farewell to cobwebs
swept with water-lights. Farewell to children who smile off
into the distance. They are clouds. They are the opposite
of hunger. Their small bodies packed with pranks,
fishbones and summer leaves, the bottle-green insects
flickering over a creekbed that is no more than a poster
tacked to a wall. At night, the creek lures animals
to drink. It drinks all the stars.

The birds have disappeared into trees, a troubling quiet.
You feel the loose mirrors around you, a forest of
water. Lakes sway in your chest. Will you starve
in such drench and coldness, be choked with distaste?
You could stand here for hours and then turn to
storm—sheer refusal and will. You could collapse
into fear and draw back into foam. These sheets of rain
are fences and crops, deeds, statues, ponds.
They are things you can't change. Things you can't say.

But you are unscathed. The delicate grasslands
have thinned to sound traveling across miles
of white dust. The rustling of stalks and small wings
into incandescent violet air. The wrongs done to you
are nothing, every sign is a proof—your feet locked
to the cinder crater, your arms thrown open in vast
magnetic charge. You are pure flute, pure iron and luster,
you are the lights of the deep drawn to surface
coolness. You have become everything you needed
to become, without regret speech or movement.
There is only night falling. There is no chance of error.

We were weightless, abalone, pulses strung into sun.
We were gentle and parched, our hands tangled in
twine. We slept on linen or straw, held cast-iron
pans that were spinning with flame. And fed each other.
And refused to offer food. How much darkness
was in us, how much green silt-sifted night?
Drawn together by gravity, we held to our frames,
clung to duration, wept when we lost. We understood
we were here for a reason but could not tell
what that was. Between awareness and stillness we saw
someone crawling, someone laughing. And chose.

Quiet, liquid pearl. Glassblown lunar stillness.
The moon rising over the walls we helplessly build.
Trying to cross, bodies fold in the fields, and sometimes
we rush to them through the gray lights of dawn. Moon-
blindness sits in us. We are vast afterthoughts, bristling
stewards of flight. Under such flooding light, you may be
small and plainspoken but you have always been straw,
musk, you have always been floating ribs laced together in full
breath and charge. First ask: who am I. Then stand and go.

And sometimes sky, falling through scales of color,
lifts our eyes enough to see. A tree packed with starlings
explodes in spectral dawn. Rain breaks across a road,
curtains of seed-pearls. Your ear picks up a cry—
animal or man. What we have taken from other lives
flashes from black quartz and sifts through
highway mist dissolved by noon. Blink
and it returns in the blown glass of clouds, the cool
threaded sound of water running. Crushing beauty
is laid every day without scorn at your feet.

Desert heat rippling the dusk, neon-tufted
weeds against luminous blue. You have stood
and watched the safety in you scatter. Softening ice,
carbon, pressure—close your eyes they do not vanish.
Still, there are kinships of air, fountains sprung
from fractures in earth, small veins of gold.
Whole flocks floating over your hands. This is
the breathable world, which can be summoned.
You do no more than feel what you have.

There is no almanac for the living—a pulse flies
and then stops. You are pain pinned to muscle—
also grasses, breath, tree-dawns, and gears.
You are dark arteries of quiet, the white heat
smashed through deserts and levers and coasts—
that flickering pause between thoughts. More even
than your own life, you flow from what is.
The stars swept into stillness, the ground drinking
rain. You are the whole shape of sound.
Whether or not you sing.

We seek the dark—certain things we reveal
only in the dark. Musk, flying clouds.
A breath spoken into the eyelids
of the one most close to you.

Dusk, electrical veil, a mist of light hanging over
the desert. On foot you are subdued, no less a form
than a fence, or that dry husk of pine. What hollowness
you live with flows out into dust and low gold-gray
stalks. As you walk, under nightrise, you will be the first
whose eyes range across radio waves into the colors
of just a few stars. You have been here before,
merely listening. What you feared most was already
brought back to you, through quiet, without force or pain.

Against the white walls, black shadow-wisps of circling
birds. Bits of ash carried on currents carried on stone.
If the wind is right, the sounds of a river become
a rushing chord, then an insect netting-of-wings, faint-beating
pulse at the wrist. We breathe, and then are gone—
disappeared into land, whose volcanic glass
feels cool to the touch. And is black, and is astral.

They were never yours. The evenings were
never yours. The river's opal stones. Rain thrown
against the current as cities rose into the red
dark. Their arches and grids belong to no one.
But the faces denied entrance are yours, the weak ones
are yours, lamentations and anthems streaking through
your veins, dark with sleet and thaw. Every effort,
every desire that began in you must change course,
the snowflakes blowing for hours, gray
but still burning. You touch hidden stars
as you turn the pages of a book that cannot end.
A sense of silence and light places itself in your hands.

Long days. Inside your ribcage the last minutes of
daylight still linger, breath and silver through the darkening
blue. We go a long way to take hold of ourselves,
dreaming and acting. Dusk falling on water. A few flowers
survive snowpack, a few fields turned over in farms.
Night blows for a while through the veindark trees
as the tree-roots shift underground. This was your home—
strange perch, a rumor of winds, cool and hypnotic.
Every day you ended, you began.

If you have grieved you have loved. Twinned,
like the sun's thread-corona, the moon's deepening
pearl. The violent deaths of stars an expanse
through which everything moves—lights thrown
from collapse. You are coastal, throatless,
roaming through people who hold tight then let go.
You are the blue forest through which sunbeams
sweep. And you are nothing but actions of the loom
threading aster and hunger. You are nothing but roads
interrupted by wheels. What will be left in us
but pure admiration? Dust released into night.

Power lines shine from the rain, a few cattle
doze. If you look close you may see, even at night,
the sun burning against small desert flowers.
We have somehow remained alive, breathless
and senseless. But with the long ache of nightfall
comes permission to be still. Perhaps we listen,
not knowing what we even wish to hear. Moths
in the grasses by the black path. Or smoke,
or metal, the faintest scratches of night.
Gorgeous wager of our lives: it is still there.
The earth is no dream, but every day something
velvet in us vanishes. An oak's shades of wind,
sun falling in summer. We were shadows,
then shadows on mist, then shadows on water.
We were the presence that became at last no color.

Millennia. Dry winds. War crosses through steel trees.
Is it enough to hold on, under swinging darkness,
as fires wheel across night. In pure quiet, chemicals
are dropped from the air, the breath of one child strains
and then stops. This is entrusted to us in patterns of dust
on cement, a sudden sharp breeze, minerals that cloud
over with light. In the power that grows in us
when we stand on the surface of the planet, and see.

Who are we, on the ground, below the flawless lights of
sky. What have we done, what have we broken.
Our shame is nothing to the ravines and the pines,
the ice and luna moths. As they live, they knit themselves
into alluvial heat. When they vanish they form a dome
over the earth. We may hold our heads in our hands,
neither moving nor opening. But our grief is clear, and alive.

Centuries, signal flares. The crows black flames in the trees.
Who lives unto night sees the air when birds fly, touches
the ground before storms. A sensation of moving
thunder. There are whole nights of snow. We will lose
this too—we will lose everything. But fiercely, in the dark.

Underground fountains and grottos, hallways
once lit by fires. Through the opening in the dome,
sun falls on ancient stone. If you stand, eyes lifted,
your life might pass across it—swift, like a bird, or a few
slow clouds. You have tried hard to hold on,
to make sense, your thoughts always whirring to light.
High above you, among the grass and ruins, crocuses
are closing, an old man on a park bench has slept.
This may matter more than anything you have
fought for, anything you have desired, or had to leave.

Dark blue, bronze-flickering stars, the sky color
deep against the volcanic field. A quiet made of moths
and water. Even here your arms fly up to shield
your eyes. What you did, what you said, what stung you.
It gets harder to live—the losses more thorough,
more painful, borne in your chest along the roads.
The shift to peace is soft, barely there.
A scrape of gravel, the breathing of trees.

It is easy to despair, easiest for those who live with
constant desertion. Where should we find ourselves,
drawing back from a murderous world.
Sheets of green fields, the first dark drops of rain.
What does it mean to go on. What does it mean
to have never felt at home. Ground of dusts,
hunger and dry heat, how shall we look
beyond ourselves, beyond the humiliations of men.
A thousand clouded eyes. Trust, when it returns,
returns for no reason. A train-horn at night.
A swallow deep in the sky.

Hammered copper. Heirlooms and winter photographs,
the deep wear of ore. There is no far country. You will know
to draw close to certain laughters, certain lights in the eyes
of men and women that blaze past their frames.
Whatever they touch is increased. They live past suffering.
Time of the great light of possession, ice and years.
Time of dust. Time of snow falling on roads.

Ankerite glints in the ground, the evening rises.
Those you consider your enemies also wonder *What for*.
You merely lived. You were offered the ice-crushed
movement of rivers, gravel roads, hawks with fields
in their eyes. Years, alluvial soils—which can be broken.
The great herds crossing the plains drove past
their hunger. These are the hands that trace the bark
or catch the soft rain blown in by clouds. These are
the exhausted sleeping men. Welcome and farewell.

It is late, but the darkness breaks open. Mercy
grows in you. The green fires of night burn through
the same air that lifted birds. And this is how
a whole life unfolds—in minutes too painful and rich
for you to bear them. Copper roofs holding sun,
the smell of thyme, cements laced with rain.
You were a child and then a storm. You were a garden.
Even as you die you will not cease to dream.

In the ease of winds and sun, a fountain has sprung up
in you. An apple is falling. White light crosses
the grasses all day. Care of air, care of lives—
they are the same. No distance is empty. To stay here
always you would need another hour. You would need
to draw alongside the children, the blown roses, the dawns
and distant rains. Night ranges across the arable land.
We remain inside its purposes.

Black sky soaked with ghost-violet. Gold tossed
on dark agate roads. It is enough that you should
be here to see. Enough to feel the deep-floating
surround. Sometimes we mourn even without cause.
There are nights when breath fills the stillness,
days when your thoughts climb a staircase to
clouds. Carry yourself into sky. Your life is open to you.

Time of wind, time of dust, time of sky. You have
no kingdom. The ones you love will die. And to be alone
is hard work, takes a life of preparation. Underneath
the scorched domes, you are inlaid muscle, spindle-
bone, a body of mistakes—but you are turning to carbon,
sharded ice, you are the brief errand of what was
given to you in unceasing splendor. It is enough
to be the imagination of your heart, it is enough to spend
your life trying just to listen—someone hesitating,
a man with no home, families pulled from boats at sea.
Until the ones who suffer are understood, the blurred
gowns of stars will stay lit. Your torso is the sound
of one child calling, the sound of leaves in high gusts of sun.
Barbed wire flowing through the dark.

NOTES

EVENINGS AND DAYS

". . . when the sun shines through the wires / of fine, fine rain."—Derek Walcott, *White Egrets* (22)

THE DEVOTIONS

"When I go toward you / it is with my whole life." [Ich geh doch immer auf dich zu / mit meinem ganzen Gehn.] —Rainer Maria Rilke, *Rilke's Book of Hours* (I, 51), translated by Anita Barrows and Joanna Macy

"Man has places in his heart which do not yet exist, and into them enters suffering in order that they may have existence."—Leon Bloy, epigraph to Graham Greene's *The End of the Affair*

CANCER (PRAYER FOR MY FATHER)

"More rarely and more beautifully, perhaps, the profound mind in the close prison projects infinite love in a finite room."—Loren Eiseley, *The Invisible Pyramid*

NEW YEAR

January 1, 2017

NIGHT SKY

I started writing these poems after studying James Turrell's Roden Crater, an extinct volcano in the Painted Desert of northern Arizona that the artist is transforming into an observatory for the perception of time. It is not yet open to the public. I was imagining how it would feel to stand on the vast bowl of the crater and be connected to its nights.

In the poems, a voice is speaking to a person looking out at the night sky. The sequence began as scenes of deep night and nightfall, but eventually came to include a few visions, recalled at night, from the blazing daylit hours.

Underground fountains and grottos takes place at Nero's Golden House in Rome, the Domus Aurea, as if the oculus under restoration were fully open to the sky.

Black sky soaked with ghost-violet references the East Portal in Roden Crater, which contains a bronze staircase that leads up through the oculus to the bowl of the crater.

Irma Boom is making a book out of the unabridged sequence, also called *Night Sky*.

PHOTO BY ANTONIA WOLF

Joanna Klink is the author of four books of poetry. She has received awards and fellowships from the Rona Jaffe Foundation, Jeannette Haien Ballard, Civitella Ranieri, the Bogliasco Foundation, the American Academy of Arts and Letters, the Trust of Amy Lowell, and the John Simon Guggenheim Memorial Foundation. She is teaching at the Michener Center for Writers in Austin, Texas.

PENGUIN POETS

GAROUS ABDOLMALEKIAN
Lean Against This Late Hour

PAIGE ACKERSON-KIELY
Dolefully, A Rampart Stands

JOHN ASHBERY
Selected Poems
Self-Portrait in a Convex
  Mirror

PAUL BEATTY
Joker, Joker, Deuce

JOSHUA BENNETT
The Sobbing School

TED BERRIGAN
The Sonnets

LAUREN BERRY
The Lifting Dress

JOE BONOMO
Installations

PHILIP BOOTH
Lifelines: Selected Poems
  1950–1999
Selves

JIM CARROLL
Fear of Dreaming: The
  Selected Poems
Living at the Movies
Void of Course

ALISON HAWTHORNE
DEMING
Genius Loci
Rope
Stairway to Heaven

CARL DENNIS
Another Reason
Callings
New and Selected Poems
  1974–2004
Night School
Practical Gods
Ranking the Wishes
Unknown Friends

DIANE DI PRIMA
Loba

STUART DISCHELL
Backwards Days
Dig Safe

STEPHEN DOBYNS
Velocities: New and Selected
  Poems: 1966–1992

EDWARD DORN
Way More West

ROGER FANNING
The Middle Ages

ADAM FOULDS
The Broken Word: An Epic
  Poem of the British Empire
  in Kenya, and the Mau Mau
  Uprising Against It

CARRIE FOUNTAIN
Burn Lake
Instant Winner

AMY GERSTLER
Dearest Creature
Ghost Girl
Medicine
Nerve Storm
Scattered at Sea

EUGENE GLORIA
Drivers at the Short-Time
  Motel
Hoodlum Birds
My Favorite Warlord
Sightseer in This Killing City

DEBORA GREGER
By Herself
Desert Fathers, Uranium
  Daughters
God
In Darwin's Room
Men, Women, and Ghosts
Western Art

TERRANCE HAYES
American Sonnets for My Past
  and Future Assassin
Hip Logic
How to Be Drawn
Lighthead
Wind in a Box

NATHAN HOKS
The Narrow Circle

ROBERT HUNTER
Sentinel and Other Poems

MARY KARR
Viper Rum

WILLIAM KECKLER
Sanskrit of the Body

JACK KEROUAC
Book of Blues
Book of Haikus
Book of Sketches

JOANNA KLINK
Circadian
Excerpts from a Secret
  Prophecy
The Nightfields
Raptus

JOANNE KYGER
As Ever: Selected Poems

ANN LAUTERBACH
Hum
If in Time: Selected Poems,
  1975–2000
On a Stair
Or to Begin Again
Spell
Under the Sign

CORINNE LEE
Plenty
Pyx

PHILLIS LEVIN
May Day
Mercury
Mr. Memory & Other Poems

PATRICIA LOCKWOOD
Motherland Fatherland
  Homelandsexuals

WILLIAM LOGAN
Macbeth in Venice
Madame X
Rift of Light
Strange Flesh
The Whispering Gallery

PENGUIN POETS

Printed in the United States
by Baker & Taylor Publisher Services